WITHDRAWN

CHANGES IN POPULATION

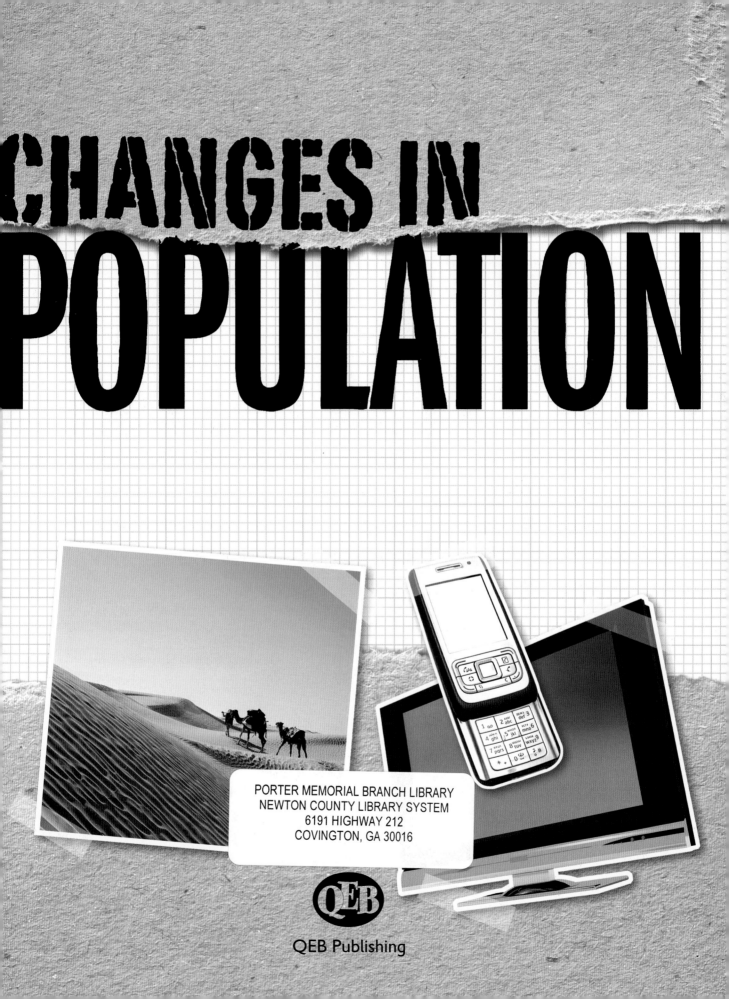

QEB

QEB Publishing

Published in the United States by
QEB Publishing, Inc.
3 Wrigley, Suite A
Irvine, CA 92618

www.qeb-publishing.com

Library of Congress Cataloging-in-Publication Data

Parker, Steve, 1952-
  Population / Steve Parker.
    p. cm. -- (QEB changes in--)
  Includes index.
  ISBN 978-1-59566-774-8 (hardcover)
  1. Global environmental change--Juvenile literature. 2.
Nature--Effect of human beings on--Juvenile literature. 3.
Human ecology--Juvenile literature. I. Title.
  GE149.P37 2010
  363.7--dc22

                    2008056070

Author Steve Parker
Consultant Terry Jennings
Project Editor Anya Wilson
Design and Picture
        Research Dynamo Design

Publisher Steve Evans
Creative Director Zeta Davies
Managing Editor Amanda Askew

Printed and bound in China

Picture credits
(t=top, b=bottom, l=left, r=right, c=center, fc=front cover)

Alamy 26 b Julio Etchart
Corbis 18–19c
Getty 6t flashfilm, 7l Andrew Holt, 7b Andrew Hobbs,
8c Wendy Chan, 10–11c Markusson Photo, 11tr Yann
Layma, 14–15c James P Blair, 16–17c Mitchell Funk,
16bl Carlos Spottorno, 18c Bengt Erwald, 18bl Ian
Mckinnel, 20c Michael Blann, 20b Manchan, 21tr Peter
Andersen, 21b James Hardy, 22–23c Eddie Hironaka,
22bl Noah Clayton, 23t Hisham Ibrahim, 26c Jeff Zaruba,
27tr Frederic Courbet, 28bl G. Brad Lewis,
28br G Brad Lewis
NHPA 25br JONATHAN & ANGELA SCOTT
Photolibrary 23br Stockbyte, 27r Davis Marsden
Shutterstock 4–5t sjgh, 4l sandra zverlein, 4tr kwest,
4–5c Ilja Masik, 5tr Lagui, 6t Phase4Photography,
6–7c Hywit Dinyadi, 6t Pepita, 6tr mashe, 6bl IKO,
6b Mausinda, 7tr Tischenko Irina, 7tr kazberry,
8–9t Kirsty Pargeter, 8l David Davis, 9l Dmytro Korolov,
9br Kharidehal Abhirama Ashwin, 11br ratluk, 12–13c
cajoer, 12c Stephen Strathdee, 13 jason scott duggan,
13l Mikael Damkier, 13br Jacek Chabraszewski, 15t Ronald
Sumners, 15c Brian A Jackson, 15br Otmar Smit,
16t Christolph Weihs, 17t Oscar Schnell, 17b Adrian Baras,
18t Robyn Mackenzie, 18t Germany Feng, 18tr jocicalek,
18b djslavic, 19t Lasevsky Pavel, 19r Dragan Trifunovic,
19bl David Hyde, 19br max blain, 21t Steffen Koerster
Photography, 21br Hank Frentz, 22tr John Lock, 24025c
Lee Prince, 24tr Stephen Coburn, 24bl Khoo Eng Yow, 25tl
Alistair Michael Thomas, 25tr Stephen Bonk, 27tr Mikael
Damkier, 27c Hugo Maes, 28tr Morgan Lane Photography,
29t Stephen Strathdee, 29l stocklight, 29br Mateo_Pearson

The words in **bold** are explained in the glossary on page 30.

Contents

Only one world

The planet we live on, Earth, provides us with everything we need to live—space to build our homes, food to eat and air to breathe.

◑Cities not only use vast amounts of materials and energy—they produce huge quantities of waste.

Our planet

Planet Earth provides all our needs and resources. Its vital substances, such as air, food, and water, keep us alive. It also provides the raw materials to make our homes and buildings, and our machines and gadgets, from jumbo jets to cars.

It's a wonder!

One world isn't enough for the way we live now. We are using up the resources too fast.

Around the world, we need 1.3 planets to provide the resources we need and absorb the waste we produce. This means that it takes Earth one year and four months to renew what we use in one year.

Running out

Every day, we are using up Earth's raw materials, energy, and other resources. The planet may seem big enough for these supplies to last forever, but they won't. The way we live today is not **sustainable**, which means it cannot last forever.

Pollution from factories and **power stations** spreads around the world.

Footprints

A "footprint" describes the effect our lifestyle has on Earth. We are constantly putting pressure on the planet to supply our needs.

Eco-print

An **ecological** footprint measures how much space you need to survive. It includes where your share of food, water, fuel, and other resources come from, and even where your trash goes to. Everyone has a different ecological footprint, and it is important for us all to know how big an impact we are having on the Earth.

⬆ Factories use a lot of energy when they make products, such as plastic.

A cell phone needs materials to make it and energy to make it work.

C-print

Burning fuels such as coal, oil, gas, and wood produces the gas **carbon dioxide**. This is causing **global warming**. A **carbon footprint** is the amount of carbon dioxide and similar gases that we produce. It measures the effect human activity has on the planet.

🔊*Big metal tanks store natural gas fuel from deep underground.*

🔊*Don't leave appliances on standby—it's better to turn them off. Many households have 12 gadgets on standby at any one time!*

📷 FOCUS ON

Global footprint

The combination of all the footprints is called a **global footprint**. It shows the overall pressure we put on the Earth.

Making small changes, such as using low-energy light bulbs, can add up to big energy savings.

Plenty of people

The population of the world is increasing. About five babies are born and two people die every second. That's 120 extra people on Earth a minute!

More pressure

These extra people need somewhere to live, and basic supplies such as food and water. Every minute, more strain is put on the Earth and its resources.

⬆City houses pack closely together in some areas of Rio de Janeiro, Brazil.

It's a wonder!

Population is the number of people living in a certain area. Some countries have more people than others. In an area the size of Rose Bowl Stadium, the number of people these countries have is...

- SINGAPORE has 60
- UK has 2.5
- USA has 0.3
- AUSTRALIA has 0.025

When a lot of people live in one area, it becomes very crowded.

Country to city

In some parts of the world, such as deserts, you can walk all day and see no one. In other places, such as cities, you can hardly move for crowds of people.

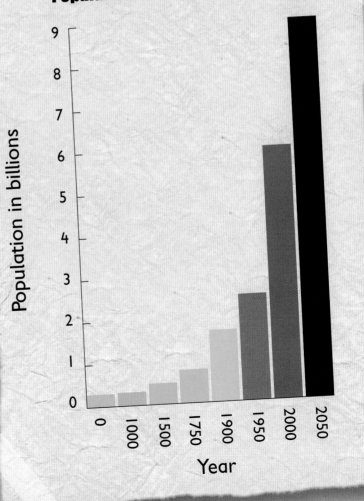

A desert is an extreme **habitat**. People who live there may use camels to travel around.

Pressure for space

For hundreds of years people have been moving from the countryside to towns and cities. In 2007, for the first time, more people lived in cities than in villages. The problem is that city people do not grow their own food and spreading cities mean there is less land for farms. This puts extra pressure on our planet to provide food and new places to grow it.

⮑ The population of the world is rising faster. It is thought that by 2050, it will reach nine billion people.

Population of the world: AD 0–2050

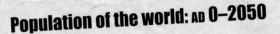

Population in billions
Year

RAW materials

In order to make products that we use every day, such as cars and computers, we use the Earth's natural resources, such as oil.

Raw materials

To make products, factories and industries need raw materials from the Earth. Many products have parts made from plastics. These plastics come from the raw material oil, or petroleum, which is found in oil wells drilled deep below the Earth's surface.

❶Huge rigs drill down thousands of feet into the seabed to reach oil underground.

Supply of materials

Finding raw materials means drilling, mining, and quarrying. This uses up energy, affects huge areas of land, and produces **pollution**. The supplies of raw materials will run out one day.

➲ When vehicles are made in factories, raw materials and a large amount of energy are used.

Metals

Industry uses metal—for example, **aluminum** for canned drinks and aircraft, **steel** in cars, and **copper** in electrical wires. Metals occur in rocks, called **ores**. The rocks are dug from mines and **quarries**. Then they are crushed and heated or treated to extract, or get out, the pure metal.

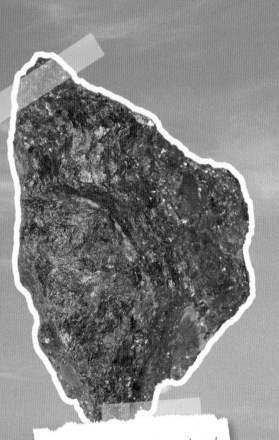

Half of the copper produced in the world comes from the ore, Chalcopyrite.

Look for "green" labels on products. These show if they have been made carefully, using the least raw materials and energy, and do little damage to the environment.

Wht Cn ? U do

Energy to burn

Almost everything we make and do needs energy, from warming our homes to fixing roads. Most of this energy comes from burning fuels.

Fossil fuels

The main fuels are oil, coal, and natural gas. They are called **fossil fuels** because they are preserved, or fossilized, remains of living things from millions of years ago. They are burned in power stations to make electricity, and in homes and buildings for heating. Oil is the raw material for the gasoline and diesel that is burned in vehicles. We cannot replace fossil fuels and they are running out fast.

Alternative fuels

Non-fossil **alternative fuels** include wood and **biofuels** from plants. They are sustainable—we can grow new supplies so they do not run out.

📷 FOCUS ON

How much is left?

At today's rates of use, how much fossil fuel is left?
- Oil—less than 100 years
- Natural gas—less than 150 years
- Coal—less than 200 years

↺ Natural gas has to be treated at a processing plant to take away the unwanted parts. This is then safe for us to use.

It's a wonder!

Passenger planes such as jumbo jets use a lot of fuel. In just 15 seconds, one jumbo jet burns the same amount of fuel as in one car's full tank.

Warmer world

Burning fuels emits, or produces, the gas carbon dioxide. This is a greenhouse gas that soaks up the Sun's heat. Burning more fuels means more carbon emissions, which causes the Earth to get hotter. This is called global warming.

Climate change

Global warming is changing our **weather** and **climate**. This is called **climate change**. Most places are getting warmer, but some areas may become cooler. Wet places could dry out, and dry areas could become wetter. There will probably be more **hurricanes**, **floods**, and other extreme weather.

⟳ *Bangladesh is a country that has been badly affected by flooding. These farm fields along the Jamuna River are underwater, ruining the crops.*

Importance of carbon

The carbon footprint makes up more than half of our overall global footprint. It's produced by our lifestyle—how much electricity and petrol we use, when we make goods, grow food, and use transport.

↻*Solar panels* *use the Sun to make electricity.*

Water flowing through pipes in a **hydroelectric** dam creates electricity.

FOCUS ON

Sustainable electricity

Electricity can be made from sources of energy that do not produce carbon dioxide. These include water (hydroelectricity), wind, tides, and **geothermal energy** deep in the ground.

GOING places

People in some countries can go where they want, when they want, in their cars. This adds greatly to our global footprint.

In a traffic jam, many cars are burning fuel, even though they are not moving.

The main villain

Cars take huge amounts of raw materials and energy to make. Running them burns fossil fuels, which causes pollution and carbon emissions. Traffic jams make this many times worse.

Green transport

"Green" transport produces less carbon, less pollution, and less noise, and is more sustainable. It includes electric vehicles and hybrid cars with a combination of a gasoline engine and electric motor. Cycling and walking are the greenest because they produce no pollution.

⌒Hybrid cars are powered by both electricity and fuel. They use less fuel and produce less carbon dioxide, making them better for the planet.

Helping the C-print

Public transport includes buses, coaches, and trains. Their overall carbon emissions are far less than private cars. Some cities have park-and-ride systems where you drive to a parking lot nearby, then use public transport into the center. This produces fewer carbon emissions.

📷 FOCUS ON

Carbon emissions

How do carbon emissions compare for a typical journey?

• Trains and coaches produce the least. The more people in them, the better it is for the carbon footprint!

• Cars and planes produce two to ten times more, especially if traveling long distances.

⌒More buses mean fewer traffic jams, so everyone travels faster.

17

House and home

Every day, as we heat our homes, take hot showers, play computer games, and watch television—we add to our carbon footprint.

Daily life

People need to stay warm, keep clean, eat, and do fun activities. The key is to think about daily life changes. For example, heating uses huge amounts of energy. We can reduce the effect on the environment by switching off heating and lights when a room isn't being used.

It's a wonder!

A quick shower uses five times less water and heat than a bath, and gets you cleaner!

Too many gadgets

Many people use computers, mp3 players and other electric gadgets. Each one has a footprint—the raw materials, energy, industrial equipment, and carbon emissions needed to make it.

☝ All of these gadgets need electricity to work. They should always be turned off when they are not being used.

Find out how your home stops warmth from escaping. Does it have an insulated roof and walls, double-glazed windows, and well-fitting doors? All this helps to save heat and reduce your footprint— and save money!

Wht Cn ? U do

Watch that waste!

Raw materials, energy, and machinery are needed to make the products we use every day. If we throw things away, this creates a lot of waste. That's why the four "Rs" are so important.

Reduce

We can reduce waste by using less. Reduce the need for new plastic shopping bags by taking your own reusable bags. Buy items loose rather than in containers. Avoid buying things with huge amounts of packaging.

A material bag that can be reused is better than using new plastic bags each time you go shopping.

Repair

If something is broken, instead of throwing it away, try to get it repaired. Broken televisions and computers can often be fixed, and ripped clothing can be mended.

You can mend and alter clothes, and make new ones by learning to darn.

Reuse

Reuse items in new ways. Jars can be washed and reused as containers. Magazines and greeting cards can be reused to make pieces of art.

Recycle

Recycling is making new products from used materials. Glass, metals, paper, cardstock, and most plastics can all be recycled. Making a bottle from recycled glass uses only one-tenth of the energy needed for a new bottle.

- Recycle as much as you can. For example, use a compost bin for vegetable scraps and yard waste.
- Rainwater can then be used for the yard, and washing cars and bicycles.

➡ Rain water can be collected in a water barrel. It is free and clean.

➥ Before paper and card are recycled, they go through a sorting machine to separate them.

FOODand health

Food does not appear by magic in stores. It is grown, cleaned, stored, transported, and processed into ready-made meals or snacks. All this is an important part of our global footprint.

Old and new

Many years ago, most people grew their own food plants and kept animals such as chickens, sheep, or cows. Today food is big business, with expensive machines used for planting, harvesting, and cleaning crops, planes for transporting crops, enormous cold stores, and factories for processing. Making and running all these machines adds to our global footprint.

Health problems

In some countries, there is not enough food for everyone. This can cause starvation, which brings illness and disease. In other countries, there is a lot of food available, so people may eat too much. This can also cause health problems, such as obesity and heart disease.

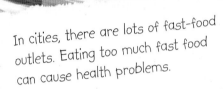

In cities, there are lots of fast-food outlets. Eating too much fast food can cause health problems.

◖Potatoes are grown in huge fields, and are harvested by big machines.

📷 FOCUS ON

Food waste

In countries such as the UK or USA, each year an average person throws away enough food to feed someone for two weeks. This is a waste of all the resources used to grow and prepare that food.

In the UK, 12 billion dollars (8 billion pounds) worth of food is thrown away every year—a third of everything bought.

Losing wild places

As we take over land for towns, cities, factories, farms, mines, and quarries, wild places shrink. This leaves less land for plants and animals to live on.

Rare animals

Most people know about rare animals such as tigers, mountain gorillas, giant pandas, and great whales. These are just a few of the thousands of threatened creatures and plants around the world. Their main problem is habitat destruction—when we damage or take over their natural places for our own needs. Other threats include pollution, hunting, and fishing, as well as global warming and climate change.

⮑ *Scientists can watch endangered species, such as the oribi, by fitting them with a radio collar.*

- Support wildlife projects and charities.
- Join an organized clean-up of a local wood, lake, beach, or other habitat.

Wht Cn ? U do

Conservation

We can help wildlife in many ways, and reduce our global footprint, too. Protected places such as **nature reserves** and national parks are vital. We can clean up damaged areas and return them to nature. Rare animals are saved by being bred in **captivity**, then being released into the wild.

The African wild ass is bred in zoos and nature reserves because it has become endangered.

It's a wonder!

Red spotted newts need clean water, but their streams and rivers are becoming polluted.

There are more than 6,000 kinds of frogs, toads, newts, salamanders and other amphibians—and about one-third are under threat.

Fairtrade

The food we buy in stores and the clothes we wear are often produced by workers in other parts of the world. We need to make sure that these workers are paid fairly for producing goods for us.

Hard work, low pay

Clothes, food, and toys in our shops are sometimes produced in faraway countries. Workers may be children, may not be paid very much, and have to work long hours in cramped conditions. These products are often sold to companies that then sell them to us.

In some countries, children are expected to work. These children are weaving carpets in factories.

⊂ Clean, well-lit conditions and suitable clothes are very important at work. These workers are in a toy factory in China.

Coffee beans are hand-picked from bushes, then sold to companies that make them into the drink.

More equal

"Fairtrade" tries to make sure that workers have a safe and healthy place to work, and that they are paid fairly for the goods they produce. It also helps people who buy the goods to realize that they can be made with fewer materials and less waste. Fairtrade is a way of helping workers earn a good living, in a healthy environment.

The fairtrade label shows that the product has been made in a fair way.

- Look for "fairtrade" labels on products.
- Where are they made?
- How do their prices compare with other similar products?

Wht C.? U do

Bananas that have been grown by fairtrade farmers have a special sticker.

Be aware!

Almost everything we do adds to our global footprint. To save the Earth, we all need to take action. Even small efforts, such as turning off an unused light, reduces the pressure put on the Earth.

Need to know

We need to learn about global footprints, fossil fuels, and climate change so that we can change our lifestyle. Education to increase people's awareness is very important. If people see an advertisement on television about recycling, they may start to recycle more, to help our planet and our future.

FOCUS ON

WWF's Earth hour

On March 28 at 8:30 p.m. hundreds of millions of people across 4,000 cities and towns switched off their lights for one hour. Iconic buildings took part, too, including...

The Empire State Building
Big Ben
Sydney Opera House
The Eiffel Tower
The Pyramids of
    Giza
Bird's Nest Stadium

Rising powers

Countries such as China, India, and Brazil are developing industries at amazing rates. Their global footprints are rising. But they are still not as high as those of people in the USA and UK. Every country needs to be aware of what they can do to reduce the effect of their lifestyle on the planet, and start changing their footprint to make a difference.

The Empire State Building turned off its lights at 8:30 p.m. on March 28 for the World Wildlife Fund's Earth Hour 2009.

◑ Shanghai, in China, now has more than 20 million people and is the world's busiest port for ships and boats.

Glossary

Alternative fuels Non-fossil fuels (not coal, oil, or natural gas) that are sustainable and cause little damage to our surroundings, such as wood.

Aluminum A lightweight metal that does not rust. It is used for many purposes such as making canned drinks.

Biofuels Fuels that come from living things such as crops, and provide energy when they are burned.

Captivity When animals are cared for by humans in a zoo or wildlife park.

Carbon dioxide A gas that is naturally present in tiny amounts in air. It is produced by burning, and acts as a powerful greenhouse gas.

Carbon emissions The emission, or giving off, of gases that contain carbon, especially carbon dioxide.

Carbon footprint The amount of carbon dioxide and similar gases produced to supply a person's lifestyle, including food, a place to live and transport.

Climate The average pattern of temperature, rainfall, winds, and other weather conditions in a particular place over hundreds or thousands of years.

Climate change Changes in the long-term weather patterns around the world due to global warming.

Copper A soft reddish-brown metal that allows electricity and heat to pass through it easily.

Ecological To do with ecology, which is the scientific study of how plants and animals live together in their surroundings or environment.

Flood Too much water in a place that usually has little or no water.

Fossil fuels Fuels made from the remains of once-living things that died long ago, were buried and preserved in the rocks. The main fossil fuels are oil (petroleum), natural gas, and coal.

Geothermal energy Heat energy from deep in the ground, where the rocks get hotter as you go deeper.

Global footprint A combination of carbon footprint, ecological footprint, and other footprints. It shows the overall pressure that people's lifestyles put on Earth.

Global warming The rise in the temperature of the atmosphere. It is caused by increased amounts of greenhouse gases, which are produced when burning fuels.

Greenhouse gas A gas that traps the Sun's heat and makes the atmosphere around the Earth warmer.

Habitat A particular kind of place where animals and plants live, such as a river, wood, desert, or coral reef.

Hurricane A large powerful storm with fast winds that swirl round and lots of heavy rain.

Hydroelectric When electricity is made using moving water.

Nature reserve A place that is protected or set aside for wildlife to live freely, without being threatened by people.

Ore A rock that contains metal.

Pollution When harmful substances such as chemicals or trash get into the surroundings and cause damage.

Power station A building that has machines called generators to make electricity.

Quarry A place where rocks are dug out of the ground.

Solar panels Special panels that use the heat and light of the Sun to create solar energy.

Steel A hard, strong metal that contains mainly iron and small amounts of carbon.

Sustainable Something that willl not run out.

Weather Conditions such as the temperature, amount of rain, and wind strength, and how these conditions change from day to day and week to week.

Index